It Is Red

by Joanna Lake

OXFORD
UNIVERSITY PRESS

Pick the socks up.

Put the socks in.

It is red.

It is up on top.

Get the pot and pan.

Pop it into the pan.

Dad gets the dim sum.

I go to Nan.

It is a red packet.

I go to Dad.

Encourage students to use the images to review the topic.